French
Bistro
COOKING

A QUANTUM BOOK

Published by
Chartwell Books
A Division of Book Sales, Inc.
114 Northfield Avenue
Edison, New Jersey, 08837
USA

ISBN 0-7858-0671-7

This book was produced by
Quantum Books Ltd
6 Blundell Street
London N7 9BH

Produced in Australia by Griffin Colour

French Bistro COOKING

JOHN VARNOM

CHARTWELL
BOOKS, INC.

Thick Carrot Soup Crécy Style
SOUPE CRECY

SERVES 6
Cooking time 1½ hours
INGREDIENTS
¼ lb lean unsmoked bacon
1 medium onion
2¼ lb carrots
10 cups stock (*see* Stocks and Glazes)
½ cup heavy cream
Salt and pepper to taste

PREPARATION

▪ Dice the bacon and the onion and sweat both together over low heat for about 10 minutes. As the bacon and onions are cooking slice the carrots finely.
▪ Add the carrots to the mixture, cover and cook for a further 10 minutes at the same low heat.
▪ Add the stock, cover and simmer for 1 hour.
▪ Press the mixture through a fine strainer or liquidize, then return to the heat. Whisk in the cream, season and serve immediately.

CHEF'S ASIDE

Anything *de Crécy* denotes the presence of carrots, for Crécy is a northern French town famous for its carrots. This is a mark of distinction in an area of mixed rural economy, not unlike a small stretch of sea being famous for its water.

Provençal Fish Soup

SOUPE DE POISSON PROVENÇALE

SERVES 6
Cooking time 1 hour
INGREDIENTS
1 lb white fish trimmings
1 large onion
2 tbsp chopped parsley
2 bay leaves
Juice of 1 lemon
10 white peppercorns
¾ cup tomato paste
2 tbsp paprika
1 pinch saffron or turmeric
Salt and pepper to taste

PREPARATION

■ Put the fish, the onion, peeled and halved, the parsley, bay leaves, lemon juice and white wine into 5 pt water and bring to a boil. Turn down the heat and simmer gently for 25–30 minutes.

■ Add the peppercorns and let the broth stand for 5 minutes or so. Strain, discard all the debris and replace the broth on high heat.

■ Add the tomato paste, paprika and saffron or turmeric. Reduce the broth by one-third. Season to taste with salt and pepper. This soup can be made ahead and reheated – this also gives the flavors time to combine and mature.

COOK'S TIPS

This soup is traditionally served with three accompaniments which, as accompaniments go, are among the most inspired in the French kitchen. They are:

Rouille, a mayonnaise strongly flavored with cayenne pepper and garlic and colored with paprika (*see* Mayonnaise). Toasted French bread. Grated Gruyère cheese. You are not getting a recipe for these latter two items. But you are getting a wine recommendation: chilled rosé, preferably from Provence.

Cold Vegetables in White Wine, Olive Oil, Lemon and Parsley

LEGUMES A LA GRECQUE

SERVES 2–22

Cooking time 20 minutes
minimum

INGREDIENTS

⅔ cup white wine

⅓ cup olive oil

1 sprig parsley, finely chopped

⅔ cup water

Juice of 1 lemon

1 bay leaf

6 black peppercorns

Salt to taste

Selection of fresh vegetables

PREPARATION

■ *Blanch your choice of vegetables and dress them in the marinade (see Cook's Tips).*

BLANCHING TABLE		
Asparagus	tips only	8 minutes
Eggplants	do not use	
Broccoli	flowerets	2 minutes
Carrots	batons	3 minutes
Cauliflower	flowerets	4 minutes
Zucchini	batons	do not blanch
Fennel	diced	6 minutes
Green beans	whole	5 minutes
Snow peas	whole	1 minute
Mushrooms	sliced	do not blanch
Onions	sliced	4 minutes
Peppers	sliced	4 minutes
Root vegetables	small dice	4 minutes

COOK'S TIPS

All vegetables suit this dish, except anything from the cabbage family or highly-dyed vegetables such as beets, whose colors will run. The following table shows the cuts and blanching times for the selection you will be most likely to use – or find, if it comes to that. Blanch in boiling, salted water.

Warm Salad of Sweetcorn and Chicken Livers

SALADE TIEDE BRESSANE

SERVES 4

Cooking time 5 minutes

INGREDIENTS

4½ tbsp walnut oil

2 tbsp butter

8 chicken livers

⅔ cup corn

1 frisée lettuce

1 head of argula

4½ tbsp vinaigrette
(see Vinaigrette)

Salt and pepper to taste

PREPARATION

▓ Amalgamate the oil and butter in a skillet over high heat. Toss in the chicken livers and saute for 3 minutes on each side. Add the corn and remove the pan from the heat.

▓ Arrange the frisée and the argula prettily on each plate and lightly season with the salt and pepper.

▓ Add the vinaigrette to the still warm pan and scrape to combine with the pan juices. Dress each salad with two of the chicken livers, pour over half of the pan juices and the corn, and serve immediately.

Snails in their Shells with Garlic and Parsley Butter

ESCARGOTS À LA BOURGUIGNONNE

SERVES 4
(1 DOZEN EACH)

Cooking time 5–6 minutes

Oven temperature 400°F

INGREDIENTS

½ lb butter

5 tbsp finely chopped garlic cloves

2 tbsp chopped parsley

2 small chopped shallots

Salt and pepper to taste

48 prepared snails (see Cook's Tips)

PREPARATION

▨ Well in advance of the meal, prepare the snails as follows:

▨ Starve the live snails for 3 weeks or cover them for 24 hours with coarse salt.

▨ Wash with plenty of water and vinegar, then blanch for 10 minutes and then cool in cold water.

▨ Remove from the shells and cut off the black ends.

▨ Reboil for 3 to 4 hours in a court bouillon (see Court Bouillon and Poaching Liquids). Drain and clean and dry the shells thoroughly. Proceed with the rest of the recipe.

▨ Preheat the oven. Warm the butter very gently outside the refrigerator. Beat it until soft, but do not let it melt.

▨ Add the garlic, the parsley, shallots, salt and pepper and amalgamate thoroughly.

▨ Put the prepared snails in the shells and close the openings with the butter.

▨ Bake the shells, openings uppermost, so the butter does not leak, in a hot oven until the butter melts. Serve instantly.

COOK'S TIPS

Nowadays, cleaned and prepared snails are usually sold in cans, often in attractive, yuppy-style packages with the shells thrown in. Your cheapest bet is to buy a couple or three of these presentation packs and then save the shells. They have a much longer life than their occupants, especially when the latter are smothered in garlic. However, if you do like looking under stones or patroling highway verges, there's nothing to stop you doing the thing properly. Incidentally, the butter/parsley/garlic combination in this recipe is not unreasonably known as Snail Butter. You can use it as a tasty butter on many things, meat and fish included.

Snails in Puff Pastry

ESCARGOTS A LA CHABLISIENNE EN FEUILLETE

SERVES 4

Total cooking time 30 minutes
Pastry 8–10 minutes

Oven temperature for the
pastry 350°F

INGREDIENTS

11 oz puff pastry
(*see* Pastry Making)

2 egg yolks

3 tbsp finely chopped shallots

1¼ cups white wine –
which should be dry

½ cup meat glaze
(*see* Stocks and Glazes)
or 1 bouillon cube

24 prepared snails

¾ cup snail butter

(For the last two ingredients
see Snails in Their Shells with
Garlic and Parsley Butter)

PREPARATION

▨ *Prepare the oven. Roll out the pastry into a rectangle ¼ in thick and cut into 4 equal triangles.*
▨ *Brush the pastry with the egg yolks. Bake on a greased surface for 8–10 minutes or until a deep, golden brown. (Watch the pastry carefully; once it begins to brown it will burn very quickly.)*
▨ *As the pastry is cooking, set the shallots, white wine and meat glaze on a high heat and reduce by half. (If you are using a bouillon cube, reduce the wine and shallots on their own and add the cube at the end of the reduction.)*
▨ *As the stock is reducing – about 25 minutes – turn your attention back to the now-cooked pastry cases, which will have risen in cooking to about 1 in in height. Cut them in half horizontally and scoop out any doughy pastry inside. You now have a top and a bottom.*
▨ *When the sauce is reduced, add the snails and heat through for 1 minute or so. Whisk in the snail butter with the pan off the heat. Do not reheat.*
▨ *Divide the mixture evenly between the four cases, spooning it into the bases, and put on the lids. Serve immediately.*

Mussels in White Wine, Parsley and Shallots

MOULES A LA MARINIERE

SERVES 6
Cooking time 5–6 minutes
INGREDIENTS
4 tbsp butter
3 shallots, chopped finely
2 tbsp chopped parsley
1 bay leaf
1 sprig thyme or ½ tsp dried thyme
15 cups mussels, washed and brushed
⅔ cup white wine

PREPARATION

▨ Melt the butter in a casserole dish with a lid. Soften the shallots in the butter, then add the parsley, bay leaf and thyme. Allow to stew for 30 seconds or so.

▨ Add the mussels and the white wine and cover. The dish is cooked as soon as steam begins to force its way out of the pot. Serve immediately, or the mussels will toughen. Discard all those still closed.

COOK'S TIPS

Do not salt this dish at all. And of course, the white wine you swallow with it should be dry as a bone and simple; try a dry white like Muscadet.

Brochette of Prawns with Bay and Tarragon

BROCHETTE DE LANGOUSTINES À L'ESTRAGON

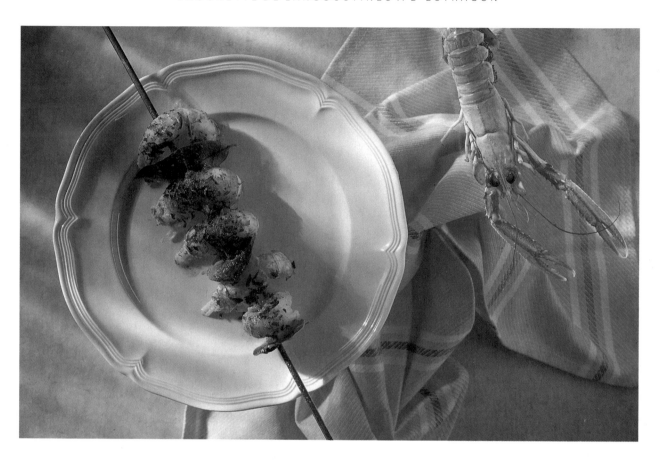

SERVES 6

Cooking time 10 minutes

INGREDIENTS

½ cup butter

36 large shrimp, Dublin Bay prawns or langoustines

18 fresh bay leaves

4 tbsp dried tarragon – double the quantity for fresh

Salt and cayenne pepper to taste

Juice of 2 lemons

PREPARATION

▓ *Melt the butter over a gentle heat.*
▓ *Shell the fish and set aside the shells. Thread the fish onto skewers with one bay leaf per 2 prawns.*
▓ *Pour the melted butter over the fish, then sprinkle with the tarragon and the salt and cayenne pepper to taste. Broil for 5 minutes per side under very high heat, pour over the lemon juice and serve.*

COOK'S TIP

You may not naturally associate tarragon with fish. But with broiled food, it is splendid.

Fresh Tuna Braised Bordelais Style

THON A LA BORDELAISE

SERVES 4

Cooking time 30 minutes

INGREDIENTS

5 tbsp butter

4 tbsp olive oil

1 lb fresh tuna

1 large onion

5 medium tomatoes

⅔ cup white wine

⅔ cup fish stock
(see Stocks and Glazes)

½ lb mushrooms

Salt and pepper to taste

PREPARATION

▨ *Amalgamate 4 tbsp butter and the oil over medium heat. Brown the fish in the oil and butter on both sides – about 2 minutes per side. Thinly slice the onion and add to the fish.*

▨ *As the onion is cooking, seed then dice the tomatoes. Add them to the mixture, together with the white wine and the fish stock. Bring the liquid to a boil, then lower the heat to a gentle simmer.*

▨ *Cook the fish for 15 minutes, retrieve from the pan juices and set aside to keep warm.*

▨ *With the remaining 1 tbsp butter, fry the mushrooms until golden and add them to the pan juices. Turn up the heat and reduce by one-third. When the liquor is reduced, check the seasoning, pour over the tuna and serve immediately.*

Red Wine, Mushroom and Onion Sauce Mâcon Style

A LA MACONNAISE/A LA BOURGUIGONNE

SERVES 6

Cooking time including the fish: about 30 minutes

INGREDIENTS

2 cups red wine

¾ cup butter

18 or so pearl onions, peeled

Salt to taste

A pinch of sugar

½ lb mushrooms

2 tbsp flour

PREPARATION

▨ *Poach the fish in the red wine. Set aside and reserve the wine.*

▨ *Melt ¼ cup of the butter over medium heat and stir in the onions. Add salt to taste and the sugar.*

▨ *Just cover the onions with water and simmer until the liquid has evaporated – about 10 minutes – and the onions are agreeably glazed. Set aside.*

▨ *Sauté the mushrooms in ¼ cup butter. Set aside.*

▨ *Place the reserved wine from the fish on high heat and reduce by half.*

▨ *Mix the remaining ¼ cup butter with the flour and beat into the wine on a low heat. (See Thickening Methods: Beurre Manié.) Combine the wine mixture with the onions and mushrooms and bring the mixture to a boil.*

▨ *Arrange the fish on some suitable platter, pour over the sauce and serve.*

THE FISH

Fish in red wine? What sort of fish might that be? As a matter of fact, long-established recipes for this curiosity abound. You might use trout, either whole or in cutlets if it's a big sea trout. Likewise flounder, salmon, too, and tuna. Bonito and snapper would fare equally well, as would red mullet or any well-fleshed river fish. Need I go on?

Chicken in Red Wine, Cream and Mushrooms
COQ AU VIN

SERVES 6
Cooking time 30–40 minutes
Oven temperature 400°F
INGREDIENTS
4 tsp butter
1 tsp olive oil
1 chicken, weighing about 3 lb
½ lb button (pearl) onions
¾ lb mushrooms
1 medium onion
1 bottle red wine as good as you can afford to cook with
⅔ cup heavy cream
2 tbsp chopped parsley

PREPARATION

▓ *Preheat the oven. Melt the butter in a pan with the oil. Peel the onions and roughly chop the mushrooms.*

▓ *Joint the chicken into 4 (see Boning) and brown over medium heat in the oil and butter. When the pieces are brown, add the onions and the chopped mushrooms. Cook briefly together – a minute or so – then transfer to an oven-proof dish.*

▓ *Cover the chicken and bake in the oven until tender – about 30 minutes.*

▓ *Finely chop the onion and add it to the pan you cooked the chicken in – sweat but do not brown it.*

▓ *Add the bottle of wine and boil hard until the volume is reduced by half. Add the cream and simmer until the sauce will coat the back of a spoon.*

▓ *Separate the baked chicken from the mushroom and onion. Pour the sauce on top, then arrange the mushrooms, onions and chopped parsley on top of that. Serve.*

COOK'S TIPS

You should notice one thing about this recipe: coq au vin is NOT chicken braised in red wine. The sauce is made quite separately. Thus has it ever been, except in places that don't know what they're doing. The other interesting thing here is that the dish used to be called Coq au Chambertin. But insofar as the likes of us common folk no longer bathe in asses' milk, we no longer cook with Chambertin – one of the highest-priced Burgundies you can ever hope to find – or drink if it comes to that.

Roast Chicken Stuffed with Bacon and Chicken Livers

POULET GRAND-MERE

SERVES 4

Cooking time about 55 minutes

Oven temperature 400°F

INGREDIENTS

4 tbsp butter

¼ lb lean bacon

1 small onion

4 chicken livers

2 cups fresh bread crumbs

4 tbsp chopped parsley

1 chicken, weighing about 3 lb

⅔ cup stock
(*see* Stocks and Glazes)

Salt and pepper to taste

PREPARATION

▨ *Preheat the oven. Melt the butter over medium heat. Chop the bacon and the onions and fry together until light brown.*

▨ *Add the chicken liver, roughly chopped, and fry for a further 2–3 minutes. Stir in the bread crumbs and the parsley.*

▨ *Stuff the chicken with the mixture and roast in a covered casserole until tender – about 50 minutes – then remove it and set on a serving dish.*

▨ *Set the roasting pan on high heat and deglaze it with the stock, boiling hard for 3–4 minutes.*

▨ *Season to taste with the salt and pepper, pour over and around the chicken and serve.*

COOK'S ASIDE

My editor asked me to find out why this dish was called, in French, Chicken Grandmother. 'Maybe someone's granny cooked it,' he said. Maybe.
I did make a few inquiries about the habits of French grandmothers, but drew a blank. But I think what the French are getting at is chicken, old-fashioned style.

Chicken in White Wine, Tomatoes and Mushrooms

POULET MARENGO

SERVES 4

Cooking time 1 hour

INGREDIENTS

1 chicken, weighing about 3 lb

Salt and pepper to taste

Good ½ cup all-purpose flour

4 tbsp olive oil

½ cup butter

1¼ cups chicken stock (*see* Stocks and Glazes)

10 peeled pearl onions

2 medium tomatoes, chopped and skinned

1 tbsp tomato paste

3 cloves of garlic, crushed

¼ lb mushrooms

⅔ cup white wine

2 tbsp chopped parsley

PREPARATION

▨ Quarter the chicken, rub each piece with salt and pepper and dip them in the all-purpose flour.
▨ Melt the oil and half the butter over medium heat. Fry the chicken pieces until brown all over.
▨ Add the chicken stock, the onions and the tomatoes. Stir in the tomato paste and the crushed garlic.
▨ Cover the dish and simmer until the chicken is tender – about 40 minutes.
▨ Meanwhile, slice the mushrooms and sauté in the remaining butter for 5 minutes or so. Add the white wine and bring to a brisk boil.
▨ Add the mushroom sauce to the chicken mixture, garnish with the parsley and serve.

COOK'S TIPS

People do say that Napoleon's chef whipped this one up for the boss just before the Battle of Marengo in 1800. Then again, others aver that it was a Paris restaurateur who concocted the name to celebrate the win – and to move a few more plates of chicken.

Roast Duck with Red Wine

CANARD A LA ROUENNAISE

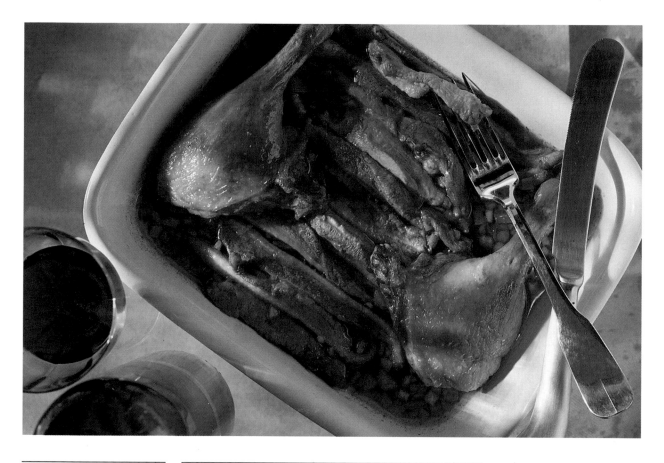

SERVES 4
Cooking time 30 minutes
Oven temperature 425°F
INGREDIENTS
1 duckling, weighing about 3 lb
1 medium onion
Salt and pepper to taste
⅔ cup red wine

PREPARATION

▨ Preheat the oven for several minutes, then roast the duck in the very hot oven for 15 – yes, 15 – minutes. It MUST be underdone.

▨ Remove the duck from the oven and cut away the legs (see Boning). Roast the legs for a further 10 minutes.

▨ Meanwhile, cut away the breasts and slice them in long, thin strips. Very finely chop the onion and sprinkle it on the bottom of a baking dish. Lay the strips of breast on top. Season to taste.

▨ Now you must press the carcass a little – it will still be very pink – to collect as many juices as you can. Pour the juices onto the breasts and then pour over the red wine.

▨ Retrieve the legs and arrange them on the dish with the breasts. Finish in the hot oven for 2–3 minutes. Serve on the same dish, straight from the heat, with the best red wine around.

Duck Braised with Turnips

CANARD AUX NAVETS

SERVES 4

Cooking time 1½ hours

Oven temperature 350°F

INGREDIENTS

1 duckling, weighing about
3 lb

4 tbsp butter

⅔ cup white wine

2 cups meat stock
(*see* Stocks and Glazes)

1 lb turnips

1 pinch of sugar

20 peeled pearl onions

Salt and pepper to taste

PREPARATION

▮ *Preheat the oven. Cut the duck into quarters (see Boning).*
▮ *Melt the butter over medium heat and brown the duck quarters on each side – about 2 minutes a side in a pan you have a lid for. Pour off the fat into a second pan, increase the heat and add the white wine and stock to the duck. Cover the dish and set it to bake.*
▮ *If you have the inclination, you can carve your turnips into olive shapes. Otherwise, cut them into chunks, unless the turnips are baby ones. Braise them over high heat for 3–4 minutes in the butter and duck juices, then set aside, with a pinch or two of sugar. Braise the peeled onions for the same time in the same juices.*
▮ *Add the turnips and onions to the duck and finish cooking until tender. (The duck will take about 1 hour to cook. Add the turnips and onions when you're 30 minutes in.)*
▮ *When everything is ready, remove the duck, turnips and onions and set aside in a warm place. Boil the juices down hard to a coating consistency. Season.*
▮ *Arrange the duck and vegetables on a serving dish, pour over the sauce and enjoy it.*

Beef Braised in Red Wine

BOEUF A LA BOURGUIGNONNE

SERVES 6
Cooking time 2½–3 hours
Oven temperature 350°F
INGREDIENTS
2¼ lb boneless beef joint
4 tbsp lard or fat
4 tbsp flour
2 cloves garlic
2½ cups red wine
Salt and pepper to taste
2 tbsp dried mixed herbs
¼ lb lean bacon
1 large onion
1 tbsp tomato paste
½ lb mushrooms

PREPARATION

▨ Preheat the oven. Cut the meat into large cubes.

▨ Melt the fat over medium heat and brown the meat, then reserve it on a plate. Set aside the pan and its juices.

▨ Lay the meat in a heavy casserole and sprinkle with the flour. Cook uncovered in the oven for 10 minutes.

▨ Add the garlic, red wine, salt and pepper and herbs. If the meat is still uncovered, top up with water, then cover and set to bake.

▨ While the meat is cooking, dice the bacon and fry briefly in the fat and meat juices. Roughly chop the onion and add to the bacon. When they are both well browned, add them to the meat.

▨ 15 minutes before you are ready to serve the beef, stir in the paste and the chopped mushrooms.

▨ When the meat is cooked, check the seasoning once more and serve.

Lamb Casserole
NAVARIN D'AGNEAU

SERVES 6
Cooking time 2½ hours
Oven temperature 325°F
INGREDIENTS
1 boned shoulder of lamb, weighing about 2¼ lb
4 tbsp butter or fat
4 tbsp flour
3 cloves garlic
2 tbsp dried mixed herbs – basil, marjoram, rosemary, oregano or chervil
2 tbsp tomato paste
24 pearl onions
½ lb carrots
1 lb baby potatoes
Salt and pepper to taste

PREPARATION

▓ Preheat the oven. Trim excess fat from the meat and cut into 2 in cubes.

▓ Melt the butter or fat over medium heat and brown the lamb pieces well.

▓ Pour off most of the fat and sprinkle with the flour; cook until it is golden.

▓ Crush and stir in the garlic; sauté briefly.

▓ Add water to cover the meat, the herbs and the tomato paste and bring to a boil.

▓ Cover the casserole and braise in a warm oven for 1 hour.

▓ Meanwhile, peel the onions and cut the carrots into batons. After the hour is up, add them to the casserole.

▓ Cook the casserole slowly for a further 45 minutes.

▓ Add the little potatoes (see Cook's Tips) and continue cooking everything together until the potatoes are tender.

▓ If necessary, skim the cooking liquor, season and serve.

COOK'S TIPS

If baby potatoes are unavailable, by all means use large ones. But it would be nice if you carved them a little into large olive shapes.

Rabbit Casseroled in Red Wine

GIBELOTTE DE LAPIN

SERVES 6

Cooking time 1½ hours

Oven temperature 325°F

INGREDIENTS

½ cup butter or lard

1 rabbit, weighing about 4 lb

⅓ cup flour

2 cloves garlic, crushed

1 large finely chopped onion

2 cups red wine

5 slices lean bacon

20 small or pearl onions

1 lb baby potatoes
(*see* Cook's Tips)

Salt and pepper to taste

PREPARATION

▓ *Melt half the butter, cut up the rabbit and brown it in the butter for about 5 minutes. Sprinkle the browning pieces with the flour, the crushed garlic and the finely chopped onion. Add the red wine and enough water to cover the meat. Braise the rabbit, covered, in a warm oven.*

▓ *While the rabbit is cooking, dice the bacon and peel the small onions. Brown them both in the remaining butter. Set aside.*

▓ *After 20 minutes, add the bacon and onions to the rabbit. Re-cover.*

▓ *As the rabbit, bacon and onions are cooking, peel the potatoes. After a further 20 minutes, add these to the rabbit.*

▓ *Cook the casserole for another hour or so, season and serve.*

COOK'S TIPS

No baby potatoes available? Use nicely shaped old ones, carving them a little if you have to.
And now to the subject of rabbit. There are practically as many recipes for rabbit as there are rabbits, which is saying something. The meat, devoid as it is of fat, is also extremely healthy and the flavor, though distinctive, is never strong. Eat and enjoy.

Braised Quails
CAILLES BONNE MAMAN

SERVES 6
Cooking time 15 minutes
INGREDIENTS
4 tbsp butter
¼ lb onions
¼ lb celery
½ lb carrots
6 quails
⅔ cup light stock (*see* Stocks & Glazes)
or
½ bouillon cube dissolved in ⅔ cup hot water
Salt and pepper to taste (*see* Cook's Tips)

PREPARATION

▧ *Melt the butter over medium heat.*
▧ *Julienne – or very finely slice – the onions, celery and carrots. Lower the heat and simmer the vegetables in the butter for 5 minutes.*
▧ *Add the quails, turn up the heat to seal the meat, then turn back to a simmer.*
▧ *Add the stock, cover and cook slowly for 10 minutes, then season to taste and serve.*

COOK'S TIPS

Watch the salt if you're using a bouillon cube; you may not need much. This dish can also be served cold, in which case a chilled Chardonnay would do the trick wine-wise. If the dish is hot, drink red.

Sautéed Pheasant in Cream Sauce

FAISANS A LA CREME

SERVES 6

Cooking time 35–40 minutes

INGREDIENTS

½ cup butter

2 young pheasants, each weighing about 2¼ lb

2 cups heavy cream

4 tbsp meat glaze (*see* Stocks & Glazes and Cook's Tips)

1 lb mushrooms

Salt and pepper to taste

PREPARATION

▨ *Melt half the butter in a skillet large enough to hold the pheasants.*

▨ *Quarter each pheasant (see Boning) and sauté, at first over high heat. After 3–4 minutes' cooking, turn the pieces. Cook on for a further 3–4 minutes, then turn down the heat. (You should fry at a temperature hot enough to sizzle but not hot enough to burn the butter.)*

▨ *Turn the pieces again after 10 minutes, fry for a further 10 minutes, then set aside in a warm place (see Cook's Tips).*

▨ *Add the cream and the meat glaze to the pan juices and boil hard into a thick sauce. Season if necessary.*

▨ *As the cream is reducing, fry the mushrooms in the remaining butter.*

▨ *Arrange the pheasant pieces on a serving dish, pour over the sauce and garnish with the mushrooms.*

COOK'S TIPS

Ten minutes is all the cooking these birds will get. They are served pink and that's that. If the birds are old, however, they must be braised, in which case follow the recipe for Rabbit Casserole in Red Wine. Instead of a glaze, you might crumble a bouillon cube directly into the cream or, if you prefer, melt it first in a tiny amount of water. In this case, check the salinity of the cream before you reduce the sauce any further. Cream. One often hears it said that it will curdle (or something equally unappetizing) if boiled. But then one hears a lot of things, doesn't one?

Pigeon with Onion, Bacon and Mushrooms

PIGEONNEAUX A LA BOURGUIGNONNE

SERVES 4
Cooking time 50–60 minutes
Oven temperature 350°F
INGREDIENTS
4 tbsp butter
2 plump young pigeons
20 pearl onions
2 slices lean bacon
⅔ cup white wine – dry or sweet
⅔ cup meat or game stock (*see* Stocks and Glazes)
½ lb mushrooms
⅔ cup heavy cream
Salt and pepper to taste

PREPARATION

▨ *Preheat the oven. Melt the butter over high heat on top of the stove until foaming.*

▨ *Add the whole pigeons and reduce the heat to medium. Brown on each side for 1–2 minutes. Remove them from the pan and reserve.*

▨ *Peel the onions and cut the bacon into dice. Add them to the pan and fry both until light brown.*

▨ *Add the wine and the stock and replace the pigeons. Cover and braise in the oven for about 30 minutes.*

▨ *Meanwhile, wash and slice the mushrooms; after 30 minutes, add them to the cooking pigeons. (Take this opportunity to skim the cooking juices if you need to.)*

▨ *Cook the pigeons and sauce for a further 15 minutes, then take out the pigeons. Pour the cooking juices into a skillet on a very high heat. Add the heavy cream and boil the sauce hard until it's as thick as you like it – which should take not more than 10 minutes. Check the seasoning, pour the sauce over the pigeons and serve pronto.*

COOK'S TIP

Strange as it may seem, pigeons have a certain amount in common with squid. Both may be braised very slowly to produce a very tender result. But there is only one other alternative: extremely rapid cooking at a very high heat. Deep-fried, or blanched, squid rings cook in little more than 30 seconds. Brushed with oil and sautéed very hard, 30 seconds per side is not unreasonable for a pigeon breast when it enters the pan at room temperature and cut into a fan. Bear this in mind.

Eggplants Stuffed with Garlic and Tomato

AUBERGINES FARCIES A LA PROVENÇALE

SERVES 4
Cooking time 2 hours
Oven temperature 350°F
INGREDIENTS
2¼ lb red cabbage
4 tbsp butter or fat
1 lb shelled chestnuts
¼ lb brown sugar
1 beef bouillon cube dissolved in 1¼ cups water
or
1¼ cups stock (see Stocks and Glazes)
or
1¼ cups cider or apple juice
Salt and pepper to taste

PREPARATION

▓ *Preheat the oven. Cut the red cabbage into fine strips.*
▓ *Line an ovenproof dish with the melted butter or fat.*
▓ *Add the cabbage, chestnuts, sugar, stock or cider. Cover and braise in the oven.*
▓ *Season with salt and pepper to taste when the cabbage is ready.*

COOK'S TIP

Red cabbage is a sturdy enough vegetable to re-heat without much appreciable quality loss. Just add a little more liquid first. Even water will do.

Eggplants Stuffed with Garlic and Tomato

AUBERGINES FARCIES A LA PROVENÇALE

SERVES 6

Cooking time 15 minutes

Oven temperature 400°F

INGREDIENTS

2¼ lb eggplants

⅔ cup olive oil

2¼ lb tomatoes

4 cloves of garlic

2 tbsp chopped parsley

Salt and pepper to taste

PREPARATION

▓ Preheat the oven. Slice the eggplants in half lengthwise.

▓ Fry them in the oil – about 2 minutes per side at high heat. Lift out the eggplants, drain and allow to cool slightly.

▓ Seed and dice the tomatoes and fry in the oil.

▓ Scoop out the eggplant flesh, leaving a shell about ¼ in thick. Reserve the shells.

▓ Crush the garlic and add, with the chopped flesh of the eggplants, to the tomatoes. Stir in the chopped parsley and season to taste with the salt and pepper.

▓ Cook over medium heat for about 5 minutes. Then scoop out the mixture with a slotted spoon, pressing out any excess oil, and fill each of the eggplant halves with some of it. Bake until the cases and filling are hot all the way through.

French Beans with Garlic

HARICOTS VERTS A L'AIL

SERVES 6

Cooking time:
beans 10 minutes,
snow peas 2 minutes

INGREDIENTS

1½ lb green beans
(or snow peas)

4 tbsp butter

3 cloves garlic

Salt and pepper to taste

PREPARATION

▨ *Blanch the beans in boiling, salted water for 8 minutes or so. (The snow peas will take only 30 seconds.)*
▨ *Melt the butter in a skillet over low heat.*
▨ *Crush the garlic and add it to the butter.*
▨ *Turn the heat up high and, as soon as the garlic begins to spit, toss in the beans or the snow peas.*
▨ *Fry for a minute or so, dust with salt and pepper if necessary, and serve immediately.*

COOK'S TIP

Brussels sprouts can also be cooked in this fashion. Blanch them until cooked but still firm – roughly 6–10 minutes depending on their size.

Sautéed Potatoes with Onions

POMMES A LA LYONNAISE

SERVES 6
Cooking time 30–40 minutes
INGREDIENTS
2½ lb potatoes
¼ lb butter
½ lb onions
2 tbsp chopped parsley
Salt and pepper to taste

PREPARATION

▨ Boil the potatoes in their jackets until tender. Drain, peel and slice them.

▨ Gently fry the potatoes until brown in 2 tbsp butter.

▨ As the potatoes are cooking, slice the onions finely and fry them in the remaining butter until golden brown.

▨ Just before serving, combine the potatoes and onions and fry briefly together – about 3–4 minutes. Season with the salt and pepper, sprinkle with parsley and serve.

Baked Potatoes with Tomato and Paprika

POMMES A LA HONGROISE

SERVES 6
Cooking time about 30 minutes
Oven temperature 375°F
INGREDIENTS
4 tbsp butter
2 medium onions
2¼ lb potatoes
3 tbsp tomato paste
1¼ cups bouillon (*see* Courts Bouillons and Poaching Liquids)
2 tbsp paprika
Salt to taste

PREPARATION

▪ *Preheat the oven. Melt the butter in a flameproof baking dish.*
▪ *Peel and slice the onions and sauté until golden. Peel and slice the potatoes and add them to the onions.*
▪ *Mix in the tomato paste, and add the bouillon and the paprika.*
▪ *Salt the mixture to taste and bake uncovered until the potatoes are tender.*

Baked Potatoes with Garlic, Cheese and Milk

GRATIN DAUPHINOIS

SERVES 6
Cooking time 40–50 minutes
Oven temperature 350˚F
INGREDIENTS
2 tbsp butter
2 cloves garlic
2¼ lb potatoes
Salt and pepper to taste
Nutmeg to taste
1 egg
1¼ cups milk
¾ cup grated Gruyère cheese

PREPARATION

▨ Preheat the oven. Thickly butter a baking dish, then sprinkle in the crushed garlic.
▨ Layer the dish with thin slices of potato cut in rounds and season with the salt, pepper and nutmeg.
▨ Beat the egg and mix with the milk and pour the mixture over the potatoes so they are all covered.
▨ sprinkle the grated cheese on top. Bake until the potatoes are tender and the crust is firm and golden.

Herb Omelet

OMELETTE AUX FINES HERBES

SERVES 1

Cooking time 3–4 minutes

INGREDIENTS

2 tbsp butter

2 eggs

1 tbsp chopped fresh parsley, chives, tarragon, chervil

Salt and pepper to taste

CHEF'S ASIDE

Some of you wordsmiths out there may be wondering: but why is it called an omelet? Here are a few possibilities for you to toy with:
▧ An elision of *oeufs meslette*, or mixed eggs.
▧ From the old French *alumette*, a tin plate.

PREPARATION

▧ Melt the butter until it foams (see *Cook's Tips*).
▧ Lightly beat the eggs – just enough to mix whites and yolks. Stir in a teaspoon of cold water.
▧ Pour the egg mixture into the foaming butter. Tilt the pan this way and that so the mixture spreads evenly.
▧ Loosen the edges as they begin to set, then lower the heat and sprinkle the herbs on the egg. It should still be moist.
▧ Fold one edge of the omelet into the middle. Fold the other over and slide it out of its pan. Sprinkle with salt and pepper and serve.

COOK'S TIPS

People do say that an omelet pan should never be washed but simply wiped dry. This is not true of pans with non-stick surfaces.
How do you prove a pan, anyway? Simply line it with salt and set on a very high heat for a good ten minutes. The salt will lift off impurities and thoroughly dry the surface. Tip the salt away – make sure absolutely none remains – and pour in oil up to ¼ in. Return the pan to the heat until the oil smokes. Pour away the oil, wipe with tissue and carry on. Once washed, remember, the pan will need reproving.

Cous-Cous the Quick Way

COUS-COUS RAPIDE

SERVES ?
Cooking time 10 minutes
INGREDIENTS
½ cup butter
½ lb couscous
Salt to taste

PREPARATION

▨ *Melt the butter in a skillet over low heat.*
▨ *Add the couscous and about 3 times its own volume of water. Stir and add salt to taste.*
▨ *Turn the heat down to very low and allow the couscous to stand. In about 10 minutes, when the cereal holds the shape of a spoon pushed through it, the grains will be cooked.*

COOK'S TIP

There exists, in the literature of couscous, the near-mythical Moroccan *couscousière*, a gadget which is clamped over the broth which accompanies the cereal. The grains are thus steamed so they absorb the subtle flavors – largely mint, chili and tomato – of the sauce below. The fact that this broth is promptly poured all over these grains during the eating process – a hugely enjoyable one in the case of this particular dish seems rather to cancel the advantage of this piece of gastronomic gentility. So we offer you 'Le Moyen Rapide': it's the one the French use.

Apricot Tart
TARTE AUX ABRICOTS

SERVES 8
Cooking time 25–30 minutes
Oven temperature 350°F
INGREDIENTS
1 lb sweet *or* puff pastry
2¼ lb fresh or canned apricots – which should be halves if possible
1 cup confectioner's sugar
9 tbsp apricot jam

PREPARATION

▨ *Line a flan ring with the pastry, prick all over and dust lightly with the confectioner's sugar.*

▨ *Halve the apricots and pit them, if fresh. Line the pastry case with the fruit, so that each piece slightly overlaps the one before it. Dust the remaining sugar over the fruit and bake the tart.*

▨ *As the tart is cooking, melt the jam over gentle heat. Using a pastry brush, glaze the tart with the molten jam as soon as it is cooked.*

▨ *This tart is at its best still warm from the oven. And when it's at its best, it's very good indeed.*

Almond Petits Fours

PETITS FOURS BERRICHONS

Serves a dinner party if you're lucky

Cooking time 8 minutes

Oven temperature 400°F

INGREDIENTS

4 egg whites

¼ lb ground almonds

¼ lb vanilla sugar

4 tbsp all-purpose flour

PREPARATION

▥ *Beat the egg whites very stiffly.*
▥ *Mix the almonds, sugar and flour together and gently fold in the egg whites.*
▥ *Pipe the mixture onto a baking sheet in little piles. Bake.*

COOK'S TIP

This is an excellent petit four base, onto which you can pop any number of enticing little delicacies.
Such as: puréed apple and cinnamon with the odd baked almond on top. Melted chocolate. Coffee butter cream. A little brandy butter with a fresh berry. And so on.
This is the end of the book and you should be learning a little boldness by now.

Crème Caramel
CREME AU CARAMEL

SERVES 6
Cooking time 35 minutes
Oven temperature 325°F
INGREDIENTS
2 cups milk
1 vanilla pod
½ lb sugar
2 eggs
4 egg yolks

PREPARATION

▨ *Heat the milk to boiling point and remove from the heat. Add the vanilla pod and allow it to steep.*

▨ *As the vanilla is infusing, dissolve half the sugar in 1¼ cups water. Boil the sugar and water over high heat, until the mixture begins to brown – that is, caramelize.*

▨ *When the mixture is a light brown, remove the pan from the heat – it will go on coloring by itself.*

▨ *Mix the remaining sugar with the eggs and the egg yolks and beat well. Trickle in the hot milk.*

▨ *Distribute equal quantities of the caramel mixture between 6 ramekins large enough to hold all the milk mixture. Spread the caramel evenly about the bases if you can.*

▨ *Pour some of the milk mixture into each of the ramekins.*

▨ *Poach the ramekins uncovered in a water bath in the oven for the allotted span.*

▨ *Chill before serving – in the ramekins or turned out onto a plate.*

'Burned Cream' Dessert

CREME BRULEE

SERVES 6

Cooking time 35–40 minutes

Oven temperature 325°F

INGREDIENTS

1¼ cups milk

1 vanilla pod

⅔ cup heavy cream

¼ lb sugar

2 eggs

4 egg yolks

¼ lb brown sugar

PREPARATION

▮ *Preheat the oven. Heat the milk to boiling point on top of the stove, then remove from the heat.*

▮ *Add the vanilla pod and whisk in the cream. Let stand for 10 minutes.*

▮ *Mix the sugar with the eggs and the egg yolks and beat well.*

▮ *Trickle in the hot milk and cream and stir thoroughly.*

▮ *Pour the mixture into 6 ramekins and poach them uncovered in a water bath in the oven. The water should not boil.*

▮ *Remove the ramekins from the oven when the mixture is set – 30–35 minutes – and set aside to cool.*

▮ *Immediately before serving, sprinkle the brown sugar evenly over the mixture in the ramekins. Glaze under a very hot broiler until the sugar bubbles and melts. Serve immediately.*

Custard Flan with Apples
FLAN AU LAIT A L'ALSACIENNE

SERVES 8
Cooking time 35–40 minutes
Oven temperature 350°F
INGREDIENTS
2 tbsp butter
10 oz apples
1 lb sweet pastry
1¼ cups milk
4 eggs
½ cup sugar
1 vanilla pod

PREPARATION

▓ *Preheat the oven. Melt the butter over a low heat on top of the stove.*
▓ *Slice the apples and stew them gently for about five minutes in the butter until they are soft.*
▓ *Line a flan ring with the pastry and layer the apples over the bottom.*
▓ *Heat the milk to boiling point.*
▓ *Beat the eggs with the sugar and trickle in the hot milk. Add the vanilla pod.*
▓ *Pour the egg milk over the apples up to the rim of the pastry and bake until the custard mixture is set.*

Chocolate Mousse

MOUSSE AU CHOCOLAT

SERVES 6

Cooking time 30 minutes

INGREDIENTS

½ lb dark chocolate

3 tbsp milk

Bare ½ cup confectioner's sugar

4 eggs

PREPARATION

▨ *Over very low heat indeed, or in a double boiler or double saucepan, melt the chocolate with the milk. Add the confectioner's sugar.*

▨ *Separate the yolks from the whites. Stir the yolks into the chocolate mixture and beat the whites until they are very stiff.*

▨ *Fold the peaky whites into the chocolate mixture as gently as possible and pour the mixture into a mold, or individual ramekins, and chill.*

▨ *Serve when set – about 20 minutes at the minimum.*

COOK'S TIPS

There are various bits and pieces you can add to this basic recipe. Concentrated orange juice or orange zest, Cointreau, cognac, vodka, and so on. Add these special extras to the main chocolate mixture just before you fold in the egg whites.

Béchamels and Veloutés

INGREDIENTS

6 tbsp butter

½ cup flour

5 cups milk (for béchamel)

5 cups stock (for veloute)

Salt and pepper to taste

Both these sauces begin with a roux, a mixture of all-purpose flour and shortening (usually butter) cooked together for a few minutes before the liquid is added. In the case of béchamel, the liquid is milk. In the case of velouté, stock.

Proceed as follows:

PREPARATION

▧ *Melt the butter over a low heat and whisk in the flour thoroughly. Cook gently for 2–3 minutes (see Cook's Tips).*
▧ *Warm the milk or stock and add it to the roux, one-third at a time. Whisk well after each addition of liquid.*
▧ *When all the liquid is added, bring the sauce to a boil, whisking constantly. Season to taste.*

COOK'S TIPS

You may well read, in bulkier tomes than this, that there are roux of various colors: white, blond and brown. This is so. The colors are obtained by cooking the roux until the flour begins to brown – a question of minutes only. What you do, of course, is cook the roux to suit the stock: white for chicken or fish, blond for veal and brown for beef and game. Béchamels are *always* white, unless you're unlucky enough to find brown milk.
And now to that universal horror, lumps. No problem. Unless truly fist-sized, they will almost certainly cook themselves out, either in the pan or in the dish for which your sauce is eventually intended. But if they remain recalcitrant, strain the sauce or liquidize it.

VARIATIONS

Béchamel and velouté are really building-block sauces to which other ingredients are added. Here are a few famous ones to whet your appetite and imagination.

Béchamel
(for each 2½ cups)
MORNAY
4 tbsp grated Parmesan
4 tbsp heavy or light cream
NANTUA
4 tbsp crayfish butter
4 crayfish tails
SOUBISE
½ lb sliced onions, cooked until soft in butter
⅔ cup heavy or light cream
ITALIAN-STYLE, FOR USE WITH OVEN-BAKED PASTA:
4 tbsp grated Parmesan
large pinch grated nutmeg

Velouté
(for each 2½ cups)
ANCHOIS
4 chopped anchovy fillets
AURORE
⅔ cup tomato sauce
4 tbsp butter
BERCY
½ cup chopped shallots
⅔ cup dry white wine
1 tbsp chopped parsley
RAVIGOTE
⅔ cup dry white wine
4 tbsp white wine vinegar
2 tbsp chopped tarragon, chives and chervil

And so on. Needles to say, cook the sauce on until the various nuances blend and, if you've added extra liquid, reduce by boiling or simmering it back to its original volume. But do it carefully, for flour-thickened sauces can easily burn.
For a complete change of taste use scallop liquor, vermouth, mustard and cayenne pepper.

Court Bouillons and Poaching Liquids

5 pt water

½ lb sliced carrots

½ lb sliced onions

1 sprig fresh thyme

2 bay leaves

2 tbsp fresh chopped parsley

⅔ cup white wine vinegar or lemon juice

12 peppercorns

To begin with, a court bouillon is not a stock. although if strained and re-used often enough – a perfectly permissible procedure – it may turn into one. The confusion arises from the frequent use of the word 'bouillon' as a synonym for 'stock.' A court bouillon on the other hand is simply a liquor for poaching fish. Here is a typical recipe:

PREPARATION

▓ *Bring all the ingredients to a boil bar the peppercorns. Simmer for 30 minutes, then add the peppercorns.*
▓ *Simmer for a further 10 minutes. Strain and continue with the respective recipe.*

This recipe should give you the general idea. Permissible variations include the addition of milk – for such fish as turbot or brill – or dry white wine. Lobster and crab need only plain, salted – some say sea-water.
Other points to watch are:
▓ Start large fish in cold court bouillon. Indeed, it is often sufficient to bring such a beast to a boil and then let it cool again, when it will be cooked, as the menus say, to perfection.
▓ Strain your court bouillon if you wish to re-use it. It can also be frozen.

Aspics and Chaud-Froids

10 sheets of leaf gelatin

or

2 tbsp granular gelatin

6 tbsp hot water

2½ cups clear stock (for an aspic jelly)

or

2½ cups velouté or béchamel (for a chaud-froid)

Seasoning (*see* Cook's Tip)

When and if you make your glazes (see Stocks and Glazes) you will discover that they set into a firm jelly very much of their own accord. Indeed, even lightly reduced stocks will sometimes set: it all depends on the gelatinous content of the bones. In due course, this will bring us round to gelatin. But let us first remark that true aspic jellies – and chaud-froids, their velouté- or béchamel-based partners (see Béchamels and Veloutés) – should really be set with the stock or glaze of the item for which they are intended.

In practice, however, even the best professional kitchens make liberal use of gelatin. And this is how they do it.

PREPARATION

▓ *Melt the gelatin in the hot water.*
▓ *Heat, but do not boil, the stock, velouté or béchamel. Whisk in the water and gelatin – insure it is well distributed.*
▓ *Allow the mixture to cool to lukewarm. It is now ready for use.*

You may flavor or tint these sauces to your heart's content. Tarragon is a common choice for aspic and turmeric (yellow) or puréed spinach, squeezed dry (green), for the chaud-froids.

Pastry Making

INGREDIENTS

½ lb all-purpose flour

1 pinch salt

½ cup butter

About ¾ cup water

Despite what is written in the Sunday papers, professional kitchens are not quiet and contemplative salons where fine-minded artists congregate to discuss their works in subdued and mellifluous murmurs. From the highest to the lowest, a great deal of swearing, shouting and outright argument goes on, many short cuts are taken and food, from scalding hot to freezing, is more often dealt with by hand than by instrument. The hand, in fact, is the kitchen's most useful tool.

This professional impatience has a direct bearing on pastry. Puff is invariably bought in, frozen. The product is uniformly good and we advise you to patronize it.

Short-crust, on the other hand, is easy, cheap and, most important of all, takes only seconds to make.

PREPARATION

▪ Sieve the flour and salt together. Rub in the butter until the mixture takes the form of fine crumbs.
▪ Add the water slowly until the pastry has a good, firm rolling consistency. (Do not over-handle. Use fingers: they are cooler than hands.)
▪ If you have the time, let the pastry stand – wrapped to keep in the moisture – for a couple of hours in a cool place.

SWEET PASTRY
▪ Add ½ oz of sugar at the butter stage.

Stocks and Glazes

PER 2½ CUPS WATER ADD

1 lb bones – fish or meat

1 onion, sliced

1 carrot, sliced

1 small fennel bulb, sliced (optional)

1 celery stalk, sliced

Any meat or fish trimmings except fat or suet

No seasoning

It is still rare to find proper stocks and glazes in domestic kitchens. Why? In the bygone times when I had a day job, and simply cooked at night for friends, I would regularly arrive home at around 6.30 with bags of raw food for a dinner I wanted to eat at nine.

First things? Grab the two biggest pans, onions, carrots, bay and fish bones into one, ditto and meat bones into the other. Get the stocks on. Then carry on with the rest. The fish stock takes about 40 minutes. Strain carefully, then keep on reducing. The meat I left until the last moment.

In any event, a preparation time of 2 to 3 hours is actually ample time to make stock and then turn your stock into that viscous, honest version of the bouillon cube – the glaze – which is simply a very heavily reduced stock. And if you're still uncertain, read on.

PREPARATION

▓ Bring the ingredients to a boil in the right amount of water.
▓ Lower the heat to a gentle simmer.
▓ If you are making a fish stock, remove from the heat and strain carefully after 40 minutes.
▓ Cook meat stocks for up to 8 hours, then strain carefully.

COOK'S TIP

Note that no seasoning is recommended for stocks. This is to give your cooking flexibility. For if you do season, and then go on to reduce your strained stock to the sauce-like consistency of a glaze, you will be seriously stuck with the equally concentrated and uncompromising taste of the seasoning. Season last, when the texture and thickness are as you wish them. Incidentally, to turn a stock into a glaze usually requires a reduction of at least 75 per cent.

For the rest, your stock, as it cooks, will look after itself provided that you:
Skim it occasionally, lifting of scum or fat with a broad flat spoon.
Do not boil it until it has been skimmed and strained, or you risk emulsifying the fats and giving your stock a cloudy consistency and muddy taste.
Expect nothing too sophisticated from pork or lamb bones. In professional kitchens, such meats should not be used for stocks unless as a basis for hearty, thickened soups.
But if lamb or pork is all you have, don't be deterred. Just skim more frequently.
▓ The permanently boiling restaurant stockpot is a fiction, by the way. It will not have been in the same place for 20 years. Rather, some underpaid *commis* will have begun it in the early morning, fresh for the day.
▓ If you have oodles of time, fat can be removed from a stock by chilling it. The fat then solidifies and can be removed from the top of the jellied stock.

Hollandaise

SERVES 4—5

Cooking time 5–10 minutes

INGREDIENTS

4 egg yolks

1 tbsp cold water

1 tsp lemon juice

½ lb butter

If you fancy yourself as a chef and you cannot make these two sauces, stop. Do not boil another egg until you have taken this book into your kitchen and taught yourself how. Buy yourself a piece of fish to eat with the Hollandaise if you need an incentive: the mayonnaise will keep until Sunday.

PREPARATION

▓ Put the yolks, water and lemon juice into the thickest pan you have. Set the pan in a bain-marie or water bath at low heat. Whisk the mixture until it thickens a little.
▓ In the meantime, gently melt the butter. It should remain lukewarm.
▓ Whisking all the while, add the butter to the eggs, one-third at a time. Whisk the mixture until it thickens again before adding more.
▓ Cook gently on until you have the consistency of thick cream. Hollandaise is always served lukewarm.

CHEF'S ASIDES

All this sauce needs is a gentle touch: gentle heat, the gradual addition of the butter and no more than 5 tbsp of butter per yolk.
If the egg and butter separate – ie the emulsion is lost – whisk in a couple of tablespoons of boiling water. But make sure you have not exceeded the crucial egg/butter relationship.
If you overcook the egg and it begins to granulate – or scramble, as we call it at breakfast time – whisk in a couple of ice cubes. This thickens the butter and disguises your blunder somewhat.

Mayonnaise

SERVES 6—7

INGREDIENTS

3–4 egg yolks

1 tbsp vinegar

1 tsp English mustard (optional)

2½ cups olive – or other good – oil

PREPARATION

▓ Whisk together the eggs, half the vinegar and the mustard, if you're using it. (Use a blender if you wish.)
▓ Add the oil in a very thin stream, whisking constantly. As the mixture thickens and the oil 'disappears' into the eggs, you may increase the flow.
▓ Beat until the mixture has emulsified into a creamy dressing. Add the remaining vinegar and season.

COOK'S TIPS

Since emulsification is facilitated by warmth, make sure the eggs and oil are at room temperature or slightly above. Not straight from the refrigerator in other words.
If the mixture splits, treat it as oil and beat it slowly back into another egg yolk.

VARIATIONS

Both these sauces are regularly used as a basis for further experiment. Here are one or two examples:

With Hollandaise

BÉARNAISE
Either cheat and add tarragon at the end or reduce ⅔ cup vinegar and 1 tbsp of chopped tarragon to almost nothing before you start with the eggs. Omit the lemon juice.
CHORON
Tint the finished Hollandaise pink with tomato paste.
MOUSSELINE
Fold into the Hollandaise half its volume of whipped cream.

With Mayonnaise

AIÖLI
Heavily load your mayonnaise with fresh crushed garlic.
ROUILLE
(See Provençal Fish Soup and Marseilles Fish Stew [Bouillabaisse]) tint the mayonnaise rust-red with paprika, load with garlic and season to taste with cayenne pepper. It should be distinctly tangy.
SAUCE VERTE
A mayonnaise flavored and colored with puréed spinach and/or watercress squeezed very dry.

Vinaigrette

The fact that this dressing bears such a name does not mean it should taste of vinegar. At the very most, use ⅓ vinegar (or other acid – lemon juice, for example) to ⅔ oil. The Italians often dispense with the vinegar altogether.

What can be added to a vinaigrette?

▋ Prepared mustard. But take care. Proprietary mustards contain vinegar.

▋ Herbs, fresh or dried, and garlic, of course.

▋ Salt and pepper.

But the best ingredients remain the best oil and, it must be said, the best vinegar your purse will tolerate.

Thickening Methods

The best thickening method I know is a constant diet of foie gras and chocolate mousse but this is neither the time nor the place for facetious remarks. Let us be serious, then, as serious as the family mausoleum on a grim January dawn. You have before you a sauce, or a casserole, or a gravy thin enough to pass for richly colored water. What do you do? If you have a gravy nothing. Gravies are not supposed to be thickened. They are best left as an amalgam of pan juices and wine, with a little stock perhaps, although you can boil them down slightly if you wish. Which brings us to:

REDUCTION

The cleanest way of thickening a sauce or casserole is simply to reduce its water content by boiling, a method with the added advantage of intensifying the taste of the item in question. Just make sure that the seasoning is not too intense to start with. And if you plan to thicken a casserole this way and its principal ingredients are already properly cooked, strain out and reserve them before you reduce the cooking liquid.

BEURRE MANIÉ

Knead together a good ½ cup of flour and 5 tbsp of butter into a well-mixed dough. Break the dough – beurre manié – into small chunks and stir it into the hot liquid. The quantity here will very appreciably thicken 5–6¼ cups of liquid. When your sauce is as thick as you want it, keep it on the heat for at least five minutes to cook out any flouriness.

CREAM

Heavy cream added to a sauce you wish to reduce will considerably diminish the reduction time.

EGGS AND BUTTER

Egg yolks whisked into a sauce below boiling point will thicken the sauce as the eggs themselves begin to cook. Three yolks per pint will have their effect, although the sauce itself should always be cream, velouté or béchamel-based.

For extra lustre and some slight thickening, you may also whisk in cold butter. But once again, the sauce must be below boiling point.

Since eggs and butter work, it follows that so will Hollandaise, which is often whisked into cream and fish stock sauces or into fish veloutés just before serving.

Boning and Other Knifework

In this highly truncated butchery section, we look at three techniques for fish and the jointing and boning of fowl. Perhaps boning seems to you too arcane and difficult a task.

It should not. Firstly, it is easy. And secondly, the results are miraculous. Not only is carving made stupefyingly simple but portions soar. Boned and sliced, a good-sized chicken will feed six and two pheasants six to seven. A boon and no mistake. But first the fish.

LARGE FLATFISH INTO STEAKS (OR DARNES)
■ *Clean the fish, then lay it on a board, either side up.*
■ *Cut cleanly through the head and along the backbone to the tail.*
■ *With scissors, snip off the fins from the back and belly.*
■ *Cut away the head parts.*
■ *At right angles to your original cut, slice the fish into darnes as thick as you require them.*

SMALL FLATFISH INTO FILLETS
On each side in turn:
■ *Make a long cut along the backbone.*
■ *Slide the blade of the knife into the cut at the base of the head.*
■ *In long and sweeping strokes, run it along the ribs beneath the fillet until the flesh is held by the skin only at belly or back.*
■ *Cut each fillet away with knife or scissors.*
■ *To skin, cut through the flesh to the skin at the thinnest end. Holding the fillet firmly, slide the knife between flesh and skin, slowly peeling back the skin.*

LARGE SALMON-SHAPED FISH
Clean these fish either by:
■ *Slitting the belly from gills to tail or*
■ *Remove the head and gills and pull out the guts with the hooked end of a ladle or similar.*
Scale by:
■ *Grasping the fish firmly by the tail, and with your knife at right angles to the skin, scrape the fish vigorously against the grain of the scale. (Do this underwater if your sink is big enough. Otherwise scales fly.)*

Boning Chicken or other Fowl

This is easy. Just give yourself plenty of time. Your first attempt will take about half an hour. Practice will get you down to five minutes, desperation even less. And re- member, your boned chicken takes less time to cook and therefore stays more moist.

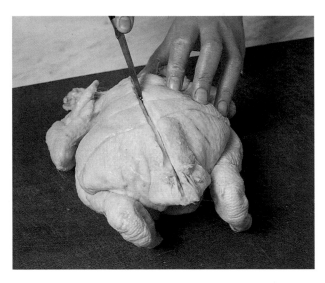

1 Lay the chicken breast side down and make one long cut along the backbone.

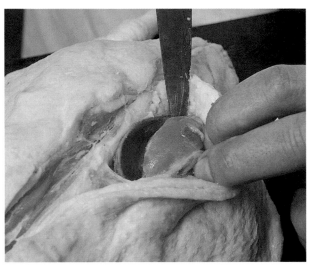

2 Locate the 'oysters', two little pockets of flesh imme- diately in front of the leg joints. Cut them away from the backbone. Dislocate the legs and cut through the joints. Holding the knife flat to the bone, lift the skin away from each side of the pelvic girdle. Pull the legs away from the backbone.

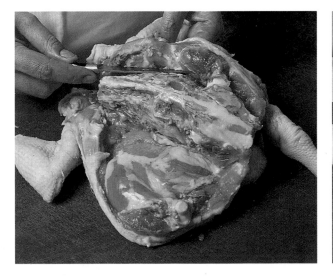

3 Now continue up each side of the backbone, scraping the flesh away from the rib-cage. When you encounter the shoulder blades, cut the skin covering away by sliding the knife beneath it, but do not cut the skin. Once the skin is well clear of the shoulder blades, run your fingers down each one to the wing joint. Move the wing with the other hand to help you find it. One short, sharp cut down will sever the joint. Sever both and continue working down the rib cage until the ribs stand proud.

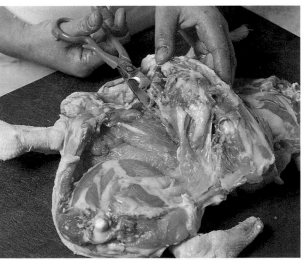

4 Cut away the rib cage with scissors, leaving the breast bone still attached.

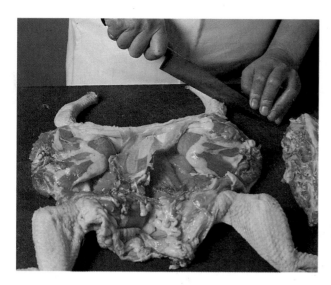

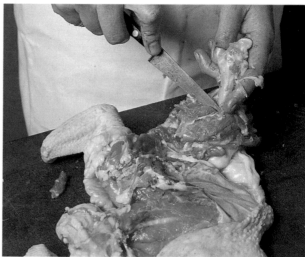

5 Now for the legs. Cut round the leg knuckles to sever the tendons.

6 Push the leg meat down to the next knuckle with the knife blade against the bone to free the thigh bone. Repeat with the other leg.

7 Repeat the process to the feet of both legs, then cut the feet away.

8 Cut the pinions away from the wings.

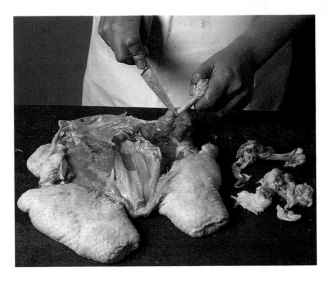

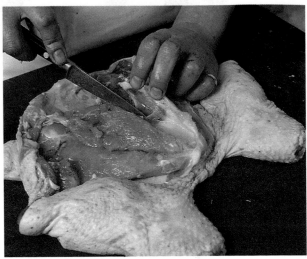

9 Push the wing meat down as you did for the leg bones.

10 Free the breastbone, gently working from the middle to the tail.

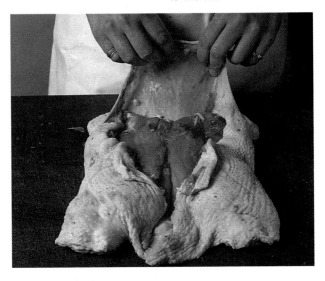

11 Your chicken is now boned. Blanket-stitch it up with a skewer or two along the original vertebral cut and fire away.

JOINTING A CHICKEN

With the bird on its back, cut through the loose skin around the leg joints. Dislocate each leg and cut through the joint. Remove the feet.

Now cut the bird in two halves lengthwise, separating the breasts from the backbone.

Trim the backbone of loose scraps and cut in two parts, slicing it at right angles to the backbone.

Take the breasts and wings and place them on the board with the breasts uppermost.

With the blade close to the high ridge of the breastbone, run the knife along the breast, blade straight down, until you meet the wishbone. Break it and continue the cut.

The breast will now fall away from the breastbone. Remove it and the whole wing. Look at it carefully. You will find a thin, crescent-shaped sliver of meat scarcely attached to the breast meat. Pull it away and set it aside. Remove the other breast – or suprême – in the same way.

Cut away the last joint of each wing, leaving half a wing attached to each breast.

Finally, cut away the skin and meat from the wing bone still attached to give your chicken suprêmes an attractive bone handle.